THE
AUGSBURG CONFESSION
A GUIDE FOR THE PERPLEXED

by DR. MARK MATTES

The Augsburg Confession: A Guide for the Perplexed
© 2022 New Reformation Publications

All rights reserved. No part of this publication may be reproduced, distributed, or transmitted in any form or by any means, including photocopying, recording, or other electronic or mechanical methods, without the prior written permission of the publisher, except in the case of brief quotations embodied in critical reviews and certain other noncommercial uses permitted by copyright law. For permission requests, write to the publisher at the address below.

Published by:
1517 Publishing
PO Box 54032
Irvine, CA 92619-4032

Publisher's Cataloging-In-Publication Data
(Prepared by The Donohue Group, Inc.)

Names: Mattes, Mark C., author.
Title: The Augsburg Confession : a guide for the perplexed / by Mark Mattes.
Description: Irvine, CA : 1517 Publishing, [2022]
Identifiers: ISBN 9781948969956 (paperback) | ISBN 9781948969963 (ebook)
Subjects: LCSH: Augsburg Confession—Commentaries. | Reformation—Germany. | Lutheran Church—Germany—History—16th century. | Germany—Politics and government—16th century.
Classification: LCC BX8069 .M38 2022 (print) | LCC BX8069 (ebook) | DDC 238.41—dc23

Printed in the United States of America.

Cover art by Zachariah James Stuef.

The Augsburg Confession: A Guide for the Perplexed

Just as living things have DNA, a blueprint of their identity, so churches have their own "DNA," confessions which state what they believe. Such documents provide the ABCs or basics of faith and tell others where a church stands on important issues. For Lutherans, the primary means of instruction in the faith other than the Bible is Martin Luther's Small Catechism. But in terms of a public statement of faith, the most important document for Lutherans is the Augsburg Confession (also known as the "Augustana" from its Latin name, *Confessio Augustana*), adhered to by all Lutheran churches throughout the world. Lutherans believe that the Augsburg Confession is a faithful summary of Christian faith, a statement to which we should adhere because it is faithful to the Bible.

The Occasion for the Augsburg Confession

At the time of the Reformers there was no separation of church and state as we have today. Instead worldly princes were insistent that their subjects belong to their religion, so that they would be loyal during times of conflict and war. So, when Martin Luther protested against abuses in the medieval church, there were political repercussions. Charles V, the emperor of the Holy Roman Empire, which included Germany, was loyal to the pope, the head of the church. His enemies, the Turks, were threatening to invade the empire and he expected allegiance from all his subjects. On January 21, 1530 Charles invited German nobles and representatives of free-cities to assemble (called a "Diet") in Augsburg in order to discuss the religious dissention that threatened his empire's unity.

Gospel-Based Reform

Many medieval Christians believed that the church had strayed from the truth and sought its reform. Unlike prior calls for structural reform, Luther sought a foundational reform that would change everything built on it. For Luther this meant calling the church back to the gospel. With an intense study of the Bible, Luther came to see that the gospel is not rules by which we are to live. He came to see rules in scripture and in life as law, not gospel. God provides the law in order to tell us that our ultimate purpose is in honoring and loving God, and that we are to serve our neighbors in our day-to-day affairs.

However, God gives us commands which we are unable to do even though they are good in themselves. This is because we are sinners. Think of it this way. If a parent tells a child, "don't touch the hot stove," what do you think that child will do? You already know the answer. As soon as there is a boundary, a sinner wants either to break it or find a way to get around it. True enough, the law is good, but sinners rebel against or try to sidestep it. God gives the law not because we can do it but in order to prove to us that our righteousness will not make us righteous before him. Instead, we need a righteousness that God himself gives us. Rendered passive before God by the law's accusations, we are in need of God's mercy.

God gives his mercy as a promise, a word which gives sinners like us new life: because Jesus has died and risen for sinners, we are welcomed into God's arms. God grants his favor and love to this sinful world. All who trust in Jesus share in this favor and are righteous. This is no fiction because finally it is utter trust in God's mercy that is the only stance that we sinners can have before God.

This good news needs people to proclaim it—preachers. Anyone can share this news, but in the church some are designated to do just that. And, proclaiming the gospel to sinners trapped by the accusing law results in those sinners rejoicing. Through God's promise, they have new, clean hearts. Given that they are loved for Jesus' sake, they can begin to love God for his own sake and serve their neighbors and this good earth quite selflessly.

Disagreement over Reform

The church in Luther's time and some churches today have beliefs and practices which do not square with this view of the gospel. So the reformers were compelled to confess the true faith and challenge corrupt practices—this is what the Augsburg Confession is about. Luther and his co-workers reformed the church to make it true to the proper distinction between law and gospel.

Other critics of the medieval church, unlike Luther, did not see the distinction between law and gospel as the key to reform. Anabaptists, from whom modern day Mennonites and Amish descend, believed that reformation meant that Christians should live as true disciples by separating themselves from the world as much as possible. For Ulrich Zwingli, reformation meant that the church should follow specific biblical patterns for worship and that secular culture should likewise follow biblical patterns.

Additionally, Zwingli believed that Luther had not gone far enough in reforming the Lord's Supper. Luther believed that the risen, ascended, and glorified Jesus Christ was really present in the bread and wine of the Lord's Supper since Jesus had promised to be there. For Zwingli, the ascended Jesus is now at God's right hand, unavailable to be present in the Lord's Supper. The Lord's Supper, for Zwingli, was only a memorial of Jesus' supper long ago. In response to Zwingli, Luther noted that God's right hand is everywhere that God is active to save us. Heaven is not some specific address in outer space but wherever God is available to save. Likewise, Luther noted that the Bible simply has no specific roadmap either for worship or for Christianizing culture. So, we have some latitude in how we worship and live.

Character of the Augsburg Confession

Since Luther had been expelled from the church in 1521 and had likewise been declared an outlaw by the Diet of Worms, he was not able to attend this Diet at Augsburg called for by the emperor. Instead, his co-worker, Philipp Melanchthon, would represent him. Originally Elector John of Saxony commissioned his theologians to prepare a working paper of the Reformers' beliefs and practices. However, an opponent, John Eck had written 404 Propositions which linked Lutheran beliefs with those of Zwingli. This impelled Melanchthon to show Lutheran faithfulness to genuine catholic (meaning "universal") teaching and so develop a confession of faith. The Augsburg Confession was written in both German and Latin (the scholarly language of the time) and read in German to Charles V on June 25, 1530. It is composed of "articles" of faith—matters which must be believed if you are to be a Christian. The first twenty-one are chief articles of faith, on which Melanchthon asserted all the parties at the Diet agreed, while articles twenty-two through twenty-eight list abuses in the medieval church.

The Augsburg Confession is directed against two different groups: It is opposed to abuses in the medieval church (some which still exist even today) and it is opposed to teachings adhered to by other Protestants, such as Zwingli and the Anabaptists. Most importantly, it says that the Lutheran movement is faithful to the apostles, Jesus' first followers and witnesses, and that it was not departing from genuine catholic faith through innovative teachings.

Summary of the Chief Articles

I Concerning God

The one God is triune, that is, the one God is composed of three persons, Father, Son, and Holy Spirit. The one God is three because God is love—the Father has loved the Son from all eternity, the Son, the beloved, reciprocates love back to the Father, and the Spirit of their love is the Holy Spirit who wants to include this world and you in this love.

Stances that compromise this view are rejected:

- Manichaeism contended that reality results from the conflict between good and evil which takes precedence over God and so undermines the view that there is one God who is perfect "power, wisdom, and love."
- Valentinus was a Gnostic for whom there are many expressions of divinity on a continuum between spirit at the top and matter at the bottom.

- Arius taught that the Son was a created mediator or go-between between the Father and the rest of creation.
- Eunomius was an extreme Arian who taught that the Son was completely (essentially) unlike the Father.
- Mohammedeans (Muslims) deny that God is triune.
- Finally, Paul of Samosata taught that Jesus was a man uniquely guided by the Holy Spirit and not God in any sense.

II Concerning Original Sin

Human nature is sinful—we fail to properly honor ("fear") and trust God above everything else and that this fundamental failure disorders all our other desires—instead of properly relating them to God, they are all focused on the self ("concupiscence").

Pelagianism is the view that human nature is not corrupt before God and that we can contribute something toward our salvation, whether our choices or deeds. Instead of being captivated to God, the Augsburg Confession insists that in our sinful nature we are captivated to ourselves and that only a thorough re-making of us, a new birth through baptism and the Holy Spirit, can save us.

III Concerning the Son of God

Jesus Christ who is fully God and fully human alone can reconcile us to God. This article closely follows the familiar wording of the Apostle's Creed.

IV Concerning Justification

The whole point of Luther's reform is based on this article, sometimes called "the article by which the church stands or falls." If sinners are to be righteous before God it will only be because God forgives them for Jesus' sake. Jesus died for us, taking away our sin and death, so that we might have eternal life. God declares that all who trust in Jesus for their salvation are righteous in his sight.

V. Concerning the Office of Preaching

God's declaration of forgiveness and new life needs an ambassador, a preacher. Since we are bodily creatures (and not disembodied spirits), God uses physical means to bring this good news to us—preaching heard through our ears, baptism as a drowning of our old nature, and the Lord's Supper which gives us the risen Jesus and his forgiveness, life, and salvation with the bread and wine. God works through means, and has established an office—that of preaching—whose role it is to administer this grace.

VI Concerning the New Obedience

The faith which the Holy Spirit works in our hearts issues in an active life of service. Good fruit comes from a good tree. Passive before God and receivers of his grace, we are ever active in the world serving as "little Christs" (as Luther put it) to our neighbors.

VII Concerning the Church

The preaching of the gospel results in an assembly of believers, the church. This one holy Christian Church is found where the gospel is purely preached and the sacraments properly administered. Nothing else is required to make the church be the church. The true church tolerates some differences of how it is governed as well as some ceremonies.

VIII What Is the Church?

The church is the collection of believers who trust the promise declared in word and sacrament. Yet, the church is never free of hypocrites and public sinners. Nevertheless the word and sacraments remain valid because they are instituted by Christ. Their validity is not dependent on the character of the pastor.

IX Concerning Baptism

Baptism is necessary for salvation and God offers grace through baptism. Baptism is available to all sinners, including children. Its power is not governed by our decisions and thinking.

X Concerning the Lord's Supper

Unlike Zwingli's view that the Lord's Supper as a memorial, the Lord's Supper is the gospel—Christ's glorified body and blood given to us sinners for forgiveness and new life. Jesus is really present in the Lord's Supper just as he promised on the night of his betrayal.

XI Concerning Confession

Private confession is available for Lutherans. Burdened sinners who especially need to hear God's forgiveness are invited to visit with their pastor. (The pastor is obliged to keep all matters completely confidential.) The pastor will absolve repentant sinners of their sins, forgiving them for Jesus' sake. In private confession it is not necessary to list every sin.

XII Concerning Repentance

All people sin. Repentance involves not only contrition and sorrow, produced by God's accusing law, but also receiving the word of absolution that for Jesus' sake our sins are forgiven. Such grace ought to result in change in behavior, turning from sin and living for God and neighbor.

XIII Concerning the Use of Sacraments

The sacraments not only testify to God's grace but they actually give God's grace. The appropriate response to God's mercy is to receive it in faith. It is not as if God's benefits in the sacraments happen *ex opera operato*, by the mere performance of the sacrament, apart from faith.

XIV Concerning Church Government

The call to be a pastor is neither private nor personal. In order that good order be maintained, only those with a proper call should publically preach and administer the sacraments.

XV Concerning Church Regulations

The Medieval Church and Roman Catholics today have many days set aside for fasting and celebrations honoring various saints. While these observances and rituals can be useful, they are not required for salvation. In no sense can they help one merit grace.

XVI Concerning Public Order and Secular Government

Christians are in the world, not of the world. God works not only in the church but in social structures such as government that provides the stability upon which the flourishing of human life can happen. While some Christians whether Anabaptists or monks and nuns believe we need to flee from the world, service in the government and the military, as well as business, can contribute to God's on-going creative activity. Public laws should be obeyed unless they should lead one to sin.

XVII Concerning the Return of Christ to Judgment

Christ will return to judge the living and the dead, just as he promised. Believers will be granted heaven while unbelievers will be condemned. We are to place our hope on Christ's return and not on some perfect kingdom that will be established on earth when he returns.

XVIII Concerning Free Will

As sinners we have already made a decision for Christ: it is to put him on the cross. No doubt, in matters pertaining to how we conduct ourselves this side of heaven, we have a measure of freedom. However, with respect to ultimate matters—allowing the true God to be God for us (instead of playing god for ourselves)—we have no freedom. The human heart is something which is not neutral but instead captivated. To get at the core of your own identity, you need to ask the question: what captivates me? Ultimately in spiritual matters I'm not free but instead captivated—usually to my own self-centeredness.

This denial of free will with respect to God is simply the flipside of justification by faith. If God justifies sinners, then it is all his doing. We have no say in the matter—other than to joyfully receive God's favor. Of our own we cannot truly fear, love, and trust in God above all things. But this is exactly what God requires of us. Only faith in Christ can open our hearts so that we in fact honor God the way in which he wishes to be honored.

XIX Concerning the Cause of Sin

While we are indeed trapped in our sin—really unbelief—since we insist on believing in ourselves instead of God, we cannot shift the blame to God for the origin of sin. The responsibility for our decisions rests upon ourselves even if we have apparently have no choice other than deciding for ourselves.

XX Concerning Faith and Good Works

If we don't need to do good works in order to be saved, then why do them? To live in faith is to live outside yourself—in God and in the neighbor. Living by faith, you are free from your self-centeredness and you want to love and honor God as the source of your good from your heart. Likewise you can start seeing others for who they are and the needs that they have. Believers cannot help but do good works—not as a requirement for salvation but simply because they are saved.

XXI Concerning the Cult of the Saints

Given the doctrine of justification expressed in article four, it is clear that Christians are not sinners who are becoming saints. Instead, believers are simultaneously saints and sinners. The belief that some are saints and some are sinners is demolished. Should we still honor the "saints"? They have a place not as go-betweens between God and people but as examples for how to live.

Correcting the Abuses

XXII Concerning Both Kinds

In the Middle Ages it became common to offer only the bread and not the wine in the Lord's Supper. People were afraid of Christ's blood being spilled. The scriptural view is to offer both bread and wine in the Supper as Christ commanded and leave matters of spilling in God's hands.

XXIII Concerning the Marriage of Priests

Over time many Christians came to believe that priests or church leaders ought to be celibate in order to reflect a higher spiritual call. Lutherans believe that clergy ought to be permitted to marry since bishops in the early church were married, God himself has established marriage as an order of creation, and procreation is an appropriate outlet for sexual desire.

XXIV Concerning the Mass

For Roman Catholics, the mass is the chief worship service. Lutherans retain the mass but change the focus for the purpose of public worship and to receive the Lord's Supper. In no sense is the mass a work on our behalf to aid our salvation or the salvation of others.

XXV Concerning Confession

This article follows article eleven closely. In Evangelical practice the most important point of private confession is to free burdened consciences from sin through the word of absolution.

XXVI Concerning the Distinction of Foods

The medieval church tied fasting and dietary restrictions (for instance, no meat on Fridays in Lent) to obtaining merit and status before God. In the Lutheran perspective, fasting can be beneficial as an outward bodily discipline but in no sense can it help earn humanity salvation.

XXVII Concerning Monastic Vows

Since medieval Christians believed that there was a two-pronged path to salvation—those who were faithful laity and those who followed the evangelical counsels and lived a higher kind of life the issues of those who had taken vows of poverty, chastity, and obedience, living in monastic communities, was an issue. If they were to renounce their vows would they be under God's judgment. The Augsburg Confession notes that some good has come from monasticism—such as higher learning—but much evil as well—abuses on the part of monks financially and sexually. It also has been made into a path to gain merit before God. True "perfection" is to be found not in monastic vows but instead in faith in Christ.

XXVIII Concerning the Power of Bishops

Since there was no separation of church and state, bishops and priests often had jurisdiction and control over land and people, leading to abuses and violence. The only power which scripture affords bishops and priests is that of word and sacrament. Power of the clergy in government or military matters are granted only through civil means. They have no civil governance by divine right.

You as a Confessor

Our culture tends to make confession of the faith a private matter. We believe that people will get along better if they do not argue about religion. But just like the reformers were called to confess their faith before the emperor, Charles V (who did not receive it well or give it support), we too at times are called to confess this same faith with integrity and conviction. The more you learn about the Christian faith the better able you will be publically to defend and commend it.

www.ingramcontent.com/pod-product-compliance
Lightning Source LLC
Chambersburg PA
CBHW030142100526
44592CB00011B/1016